to Mariza

GW00480789

John Ha

GHOSTS OF A CHANCE

Greg!

John Harvey

Sept '93.

Smith/Doorstop Books

Published 1992 by
Smith/Doorstop Books
The Poetry Business
51 Byram Arcade
Westgate
Huddersfield HD1 1ND

ISBN 1 869961 35 8

Printed by Walkers Printers (Huddersfield) (0484 862121)

Distributors: Password (Books) Ltd., 23 New Mount Street,
Manchester M4 4DE

Cover Photograph: © Herman Leonard. Used by permission.
Author Photograph: © Liz Simcock

Acknowledgements are due to the editors of the following magazines, in
which some of these poems first appeared: *Ambit, The Echo Room, Foolscap,
Harry's Hand, Leicester Haymarket Poetry Supplement, The North, Ostinato, The
Rialto, Slow Dancer, Tears in the Fence, The Wide Skirt.*

These poems have also appeared, often in slightly different versions, in the
following pamphlets: *The Old Postcard Trick* (Slow Dancer), *Neil Sedaka Lied*
(Smith/Doorstop), *The Downeast Poems* (Smith/Doorstop), *Taking the Long
Road Home* (Slow Dancer), *Sometime Other Than Now* (Slow Dancer) and
Territory (Slow Dancer).

Thanks are due to the following, for their advice, enthusiasm, inspiration
and support: Simon Armitage, Judi Benson, Alan Brooks, Carol Ann Duffy,
Janet Fisher, Lee Harwood, Libby Houston, Keith Jafrate, David Kresh, Ian
McMillan, Nancy Nielsen and Peter Sansom.

The Poetry Business gratefully acknowledges the help of Kirklees
Metropolitan Council and Yorkshire & Humberside Arts.

CONTENTS

for Tom & Leanne

&

Liz

THE OLD POSTCARD TRICK

green glass & right on cue
the Park Avenue Plaza catches at the light
& slots it straight & clean
into the pocket of 53rd & Park

there are small children everywhere

bright & shining, they hang from harnesses,
dance across the floors of taxi cabs & through
the legs of jazzmen in Washington Square,
spill across the sidewalks like quarters & dimes;
at night in mickey mouse suits & floppy ears
they climb the freezer door,
run, open-eyed, along the recesses of my heart

we sit around the floor of the apartment
eating cheese enchiladas & drinking beer,
talk of writing & therapy
& which bands are big in the UK,
head out dancing but never make it;
no longer 'diffident', I sit in the all-
night coffee shop & laugh until the tears
turn into the three o'clock walk home

there was a time when I would phone,
wherever you were, home, as automatic
as stopping to tie a shoe

now it's this:
a simple setting-down of things seen & done
signed with love & sealed
with a shrinkwrapped kiss —
the old postcard trick

EVENINGS ON SEVENTY-THIRD STREET

Soft rock of traffic steadying down,
four pieces of chicken, fried potato chips,
dill pickles — ridged and thick as fingers —
coleslaw, cola. Despite our best efforts
by the time we walk it home, circles
of grease, dark through the paper sack,
have stained your clothes and mine,
a smear across the silk blouse you bought
for best, below the spots where coffee
dribbled from your mug two nights before,
watching the news on tv.

Even six months ago I would have said
I told you so.

While you snap the lock shut, slide
the bolt across, I am sharing food
onto paper plates; your book is open,
face down where you left it, pad
on which I am writing this poem
is on the floor by my chair.
The radio, which we left playing,
chances its arm at a contemporary
string quartet and I sense you will
rise soon, licking your fingers
free from chicken, wiping them,
to be certain, down your skirt,
before lifting Lee Wiley from the record rack —
the Liberty Music Shop recordings 39-40 -
singing songs of love, but not for me.

An hour now since either of us has spoken,
felt the need to speak.

TILL IT SHINES

We danced together.
Oh, yes, we did.
That evening and after.
  Stepped round each other,
pleased, cautious,
prepared to be impressed.

Out on the street, along the canal,
your hand moved like light
against the smoothness of my skin.
We could be so happy together.
You brought my fingers to your face
to feel the tears fall.
Brought your bone china cups
and placed them on my shelf.

Look into my eyes, you said.
Look into my eyes.

Out there at the tide line,
arms wound so close
they could be dancing,
but, no, they are standing,
this couple, perfectly still
and anyone looking at them can see
how much they are in love.

All that was in another country.
Another time. We were different people
and resemblances like memories
are blurred.

While I pored over colour cards
choosing paint,
you knew already you were leaving me
not when.

Somewhere between the terracotta
and the midnight blue
I heard you clear your throat.

Look into my eyes, you said.
Look into my eyes.

And I did.

EAST

Cold flat mornings out beyond the marshes
ugly metal shunting like carriages running track
only the buckets, hollow, held loose in your hand

In the house he has been up since four
if 'up' can be the word, squat beneath
the blankets of his chair, faint sheen
of blue snagging the silvered blankness
of his eyes

He will know when the beasts have been fed
when the task is done.

SOMETIME OTHER THAN NOW

sitting in a domestic
garden while above him
planes thread the sky

inscribed in the book
he is reading words
about angels falling
violet to the sun

he will have made coffee
in a smooth white jug
spread soft black bread
rich with glossed black jam

in some eastern european
hotel room — let us call
it Budapest — she stretches
back on the sweaters
and paperbacks whose authors
she will never remember
silk tensing across those
places of her body

when the wind eases
under the sill to touch
her shoulders
she must force herself
hard to realise
it is not the fall of wings

HOLLYWOOD CANTEEN

It seems too much of a cliché,
almost, to tell it,
but there, up on the counter
of the Hollywood Canteen,
there amongst the images
of Marilyn, James Dean,
she pushes back her plate,
lights her cigarette
and right over the juke box
she says, nineteen:

I hate films that end like that,
stuck out on the porch
in the middle of nowhere
with some cute little kid
watching the sun go down,
as though it could ever happen.
Jesus! It's like your parents
bringing you up to believe
it's possible to tell the truth
when one minute after they
let you out into the world
you can see everyone else is lying.
You try being nice out there,
just try it! You won't last
five minutes and I'll tell
you this. I haven't met a single
person since I was sixteen
who wasn't a bitch underneath
and I just haven't got the
strength to stand up to them,
not on my own and that's what I am.
And happiness, that's a laugh
and a half and one thing I am

sure of, it isn't sitting out
on a dumb porch in the middle of
Iowa staring into some
technicolour sunset!

She turned her head aside
and closed her eyes and
when she did that she was
as beautiful as I had ever seen her.

What do you think, she said, the
pancakes with the maple syrup,
you think we should have the ice
cream as well, maybe the chocolate
sauce?

Seeing my face, she smiled.

1947

down the street the radio is playing
some ballroom south of here

I could follow the breeze
up from the river
coke & a wedge of pie, 25 cents,
wasn't nothing on that juke box
I as much as remembered

each time I drop my heart
it rolls across the floor
& stops at your feet

I didn't think you cared —
explaining why you shut out the light
turned on the gas

you cut your hair short
like a boy's
silted up the bitterness
behind another man's boards

& I wonder now
what happened to that gas?
Did it just run out?
At the last moment, choking,
did he come back and find you?

that moment between sleep & waking
the movie & the dream

pick you up & carry you
in his arms
into some other sunset
choirs, kids
evenings at home
with the gramophone:
another of those dreams
you forgot to mention.

REMEMBER?

it was snowing in New York but that was Easter:
we walked past the rink where Clayburgh skated
in *An Unmarried Woman*, ate hot pretzels and
stood on line for pasta and clam sauce
(can you still taste that?)
I can't recall what I wanted for desert
except the waiter said 'That's disgusting!'
& refused to take my order. Later we cruised
the Village, hands punched down into our pockets,
Kevin & I browsing the schedules at the Bleeker St Cinema
while you went next door into the Magic Shoe Store
& bought a pair of bright scarlet boots

with wings

remember?

yes (you say) yes

LIGHT IN AUGUST

By late summer the rockets no longer fall in pairs
    but randomly
like sunspots across our eyes

At the centre of some other, further city
    you are crouched down
eyes shielded from the sun
reading

    He could not tell
    if she had been watching him

The last convoys lay beyond the walls
    abandoned
their grain sour like blisters
in the mouth. Most aid now
comes indifferently from the sky

He can hear the buckle of the page
against her finger
as she turns

    Her head was bare

Words crumble like lathe and mortar
trapped without sentence or design.
The meanings ascribed to love, children
    no longer apply

Just yesterday a family he had known
    killed
crossing the street to prayer

    For a while he believed
    that she would send for him

Ignoring curfew
he walks out into the heat of day

Sweat
salt like olives
on her skin

Like some residue of longing
it had clung to him
that at this moment she would close
her eyes and see him
imprinted
behind her eyes

She turns the pages again
    pauses
and reads on

By now he could be anywhere
under the sun.

BETWEEN

Labour Day and Thanksgiving
Christmas and New Years
between first waking
and first light
the sharp cotton sheets
in the attic where she sleeps
between lifting her cup
from its saucer
and setting it back down

she thinks of him
less and less often.

CHARLIE PARKER IN GREEN SHOES

Back in the City I walk south on 7th —
Garment Jungle!

From the squeak of the subway doors
as the train sways the tracks
cross town searching for the loop,
to the buskers outside 5th Avenue
stores hustling out-of-towners
on their way back from brunch,
music pumps beneath your feet.

Frank O'Hara's out to lunch
& it looks like he's never coming back —
poems spilling from his pockets like confetti,
heaven just a shlep away, the length of St. Mark's Place,
an evening stroll along the beach — chair pushed back,
his favourite hour, favourite meal.
Oranges something you painted, never ate.
'Frank!' The warning shout too late
to make him jump before the jeep
hit him in the belly hard and
one day later he was dead at forty,
five years more than Bird
who died as royally as he lived
each year called to do the work
of two and still that's not enough.
'Bird Lives!' written on the walls
scrape of chalk and hiss of paint
seguing into his last breath.

There's no heaven can hold him:
out on remission he scores from a dude

on roller skates in Times Square
picks up a six-pack of Coors
and hits the Magic Shoe Store
where he buys — wait for it! — green shoes!

Horn out of hock he talks his way
into a gig, depping with the Junkyard
Angels at the Lone Star Café.
Mid-way through 'Close up the Honky Tonks'
he's had enough, rips open a sack of
salt peanuts and blows them all away.

Next morning, early, two repo men
with neat pony tails sift careful
through the ashes

'Green shoes?' they say, perplexed —
'Green shoes?'

THE OTHER TRADITION

bulked inside check lumberjack shirts these stern
unbending men shift with a heavy grace, clench &
claim & pass slow pitchers between them, over & over,
hand to mouth

later they sit with banjos unclasped against their knees
and the quiet of the surrounding sky

the women move slowly round them, a cautious
circle, chance remarks, heads bending with
the wind, pies raised and, like the children,
set back down without fuss or ceremony;
cornbake bread stippled with husk of grain
& honey: the hams waiting for the men
to lay down their instruments and carve

all through the dancing — tent flaps billowing
heel & toe, corner to corner, hand slaps
flat against the knee — she watches him:
the needle finds his heart but fails to draw
him home

she knows it is over
under moonlight mulch of cone & leaf
accepts the pressure of her foot

the other side of the forest

THE BOOK THAT WE READ

: he thinks she doubts his love

he buys her flowers, silk sheets,
cello sonatas and Cuban love songs,
slim books of Chinese poetry
with bindings too delicate to touch

she finds the film of their lives
and watches, captivated; once
in a while they would stumble
surprised and face to face
into each other's arms

: he thinks she finds him boring

he enrols in cake making
and consciousness raising,
jazz dance, tap dance,
table tennis, table making,
tabling motions, table setting —
everything from a romantic dinner à deux
to a civic reception

now he gets up at five
and hunches by the window
setting down each nuance;
at night he locks the clasp
and leaves the key beneath her pillow

he remembers five pairs
of walking shoes, worn down
at heel; the terrifying
jerkiness of dreams;

asleep her fingers close
about his wrist and he knows
she is rehearsing leaving him

: he thinks she needs space

she takes it

instead of a diary now he writes poems
compulsively
she sends him trim postcards
commemorating trips made alone

in time he will fall in love
with a waitress in a shoyu
healthfood restaurant;
the way her arm catches the light
as the plate glides gently
towards him — bean sprouts, alfalfa,
those graceful filaments of cress,
their rise and fall

three years from now
she throws back the covers
to a dawn sharp and clear
across the Sierra Nevada
snow sliding down her vision
clean away

whatever it was they read together
remaindered at fifteen cents
sold, scuffed and broken-backed,
from a pavement in the Village,
pulped,
forgotten.

HEMLOCK

It keeps coming back to this:
we are sitting outside a restaurant,
a terrace or beneath a canopy
alongside this quiet street.
Venice, Budapest. (Vienna was
brighter, we liked the way
the waiters disappeared for hours
leaving us to our notebooks, papers,
strong, dark coffee growing cold.)
You slipped a sweater down around
your shoulders, pale moths jousting
with the light, and there,
between the fish and the olives,
salad thick with fennel, offered me
so much of my life that I had wanted,
almost, it seemed, upon a plate.

In the hotel I punched the bathroom wall,
screamed till both our voices bled:
so frightened what you were giving
I might really take.

This far along and it still cradles us,
soft beneath our conversations, distinct,
the scent of aniseed, clinging
to our fingers and our tongues.

GOODNIGHT, FUZZY STONE

'Orphans are notorious for interior games'
— John Irving, *The Cider House Rules*

Inside the folds of his box Fuzzy Stone has a dream:
when he picks up the phone she says she will be home
from work a little late; she arrives and there are
flowers in her arms, so many flowers.
They sit at either end of the sofa while she
tells him about her day; they have not kissed yet —
he has learnt not to claim too much too soon.

He believes in Santa Claus, the power of love,
the tooth fairy, the folk that play happy families
at the end of the rainbow. He believes
if he picks up the phone it will be her:
always.

When he was four his mother packed him off
with his own fork and spoon to find the party.

'Fuzzy is a loveable child who would benefit
from a warm and caring family, preferably one
with brothers and sisters of a similar age.'

Slowly fingering lines
mouth moving to the words,
Fuzzy recognizes himself and smiles.

Cars come slowly over the hill,
even in the worst of winter there are cars,
singly or in convoy, and when they leave
another face stares back at Fuzzy
through a blur of moving glass

When he was sixteen they gave him a new pair
of second-hand shoes, a travel warrant
and a testimonial: 'Fuzzy is a pleasant
enough young man, decent and honest,
but when things become too stressful
he likes to climb back inside his box.'

In the bus station he sleeps with one ear open
close to the bank of telephones.
There are other places: the launderette,
the air ducts out at the bakery,
behind the curtains in the camera booth —
colour photos three for a pound —
he loves to watch them slip into sight,
always when you have given up hoping,
there! Like magic. Like dreams.

The phone rings and he picks it up:
he climbs back inside his box.

What he really wants to do is drive
the wet miles till she holds him tight
in her arms (as he is certain she would).
'Turn over and let me snuggle you up.' Isn't that
the kind of thing lovers say?

Say Good Night, Fuzzy Stone.

THIS & THEN THAT

the day is full of possibilities

we can climb the hill into the city
& pass the girl with blue eyes
coming back down
camel coat like a bathrobe
on her shoulders
sleep and love in her eyes

our bags packed with spiced sausage
& cheeses & strong with the smell
of fresh coffee
we sit and eat a slow, late breakfast
you read one of the folded papers
while I wait a little breathless
for the waitress to dip low
skirt peeling back from her legs
like fine blue paint

you stop me with a smile

Dave gets up from piano practice —
tousle-haired kids draw men like stars —
we talk of Rothko, Frank O'Hara, the blues:
Gill out, getting on with life

later take the cat for a walk
round the park
check out the evening's movies —
I can tell from the look in your eyes
we'll be in bed soon

sunset back of the trees

GRACE NOTES

Let us say it has been one of those
insubstantial inner-city days,
from the humid flower beds of the park
to the slim-hipped cellist
playing the inevitable Bach.

And say, strolling home, I chance to pass
this bar just hours after David Murray
has jet-lagged in from New York.
It's light enough still for the doors
to be open out onto the street;
the sound and the small crowd
draw me inside and there on stage
before bass and drums he stands:
back arched, chest pigeoned forward,
horn angled outwards as he rocks
lightly back from heel to toe,
toeing the line of a calypso so true,
the crowd, as one, leans back and smiles,
relaxed, not noticing those heels
have lifted with an extra bounce
and before anyone can drink or think
his left leg kicks out in the peerless curve
of a high hurdler; the tenor twists and soars
and lifts us, holds us to him, wrapt
in curlicues of sound, blessed
by the effortless grace of his playing.

Finished, he steps off stage and I don't
know what to do with all this silence,
except from nowhere I am thinking of you,
your mouth, the fineness of your hair,

hazel switch of colour in your eyes,
your mouth again, the way you stand
a little to one side and cock your head
and stare, swell of your belly, hot
against my face, perfection of your breasts,
your back, your smile . . .

God! You are beautiful!

CHET BAKER

looks out from his hotel room
across the Amstel to the girl
cycling by the canal who lifts
her hand and waves and when
she smiles he is back in times
when every Hollywood producer
wanted to turn his life
into that bitter-sweet story
where he falls badly, but only
in love with Pier Angeli,
Carol Lynley, Natalie Wood;
that day he strolled into
the studio, fall of fifty-two,
and played those perfect lines
across the chords of 'Funny Valentine'
and now when he looks from his window
and her passing smile up to the blue
of a perfect sky he knows
this is one of those rare days
when he can truly fly.

HEART-WHOLE

adj. rare : not in love

Casaubon advertised in the New Statesman:
Fiftyish academic, interested in biblical exegesis
cold baths and the films of Carl Dreyer
seeks young woman to share life's work.
Non-smoker essential. C of E preferred.

The only answer from a Doctor Chillingworth
struck off in America, practising
acupuncture in Muswell Hill.

They meet alternate Tuesdays
in the side room of a pub
and talk of guilt and scholarship and sin
Hester and Dorothea
and things that might have been.

Lest he become too comfortable
Casaubon wears shoes a size
too small, laced tight,
writes crabbed words
long into the night.

It was not so wild a dream, —
old as I was, and sombre as I was, —
and misshapen as I was, —
that the simple bliss,
which is scattered far and wide,
for all mankind to gather up,
might yet be mine.

Chillingworth, Casaubon and I
tempters of freshman girls
flaunting our decay in tight jeans
bulging temples and eyes.

We sit in seminars and trains
thesis papers spread before us
catch taxis from wrong destinations
to where you wait anxiously
at stations, coffee shops
and stops along the motorway,
talk or don't talk, wait
for you to make your move,
tell all until you cry.

> *Thou knowest I was frank with thee.*
> *I felt no love nor feigned any.*

No love: that much you understand.
Our work must have first claim.

We warm ourselves on your bodies
feed on your skin.

You remove your rings
and lay them neatly down;
I keep one eye on the clock,
one finger across my heart.

MAKING MAPS

for Tom

Pushing up from Browning
through the Blackfeet Reservation
white crosses at the roadside
in fives & sixes now,
broken-down pick-ups
dead in the back yards
of broken shacks

We grin as 'All Shook Up'
grinds out from the radio
lean our heads close and
sing as hard as we can

Driving through England
memory surprises me

I have been trying to write about this
for a long time now

Sarah drove with us from the airport,
slowing as we passed a grain elevator
bulked against the sky:
'Used to map my way round
Montana counting those . . .'

You made dams wherever we went:
crouched patient over small streams
all the way from Castle to Iceberg
Lake, stopping time with your hands

When the deer breathed down
through trees to the salt lick
at dusk I reckoned you'd earned it

Storms and rainbows
surrounded us

We drove through three states
three thousand miles
& love drove us fast together.

THE FIRST DAY OF SUMMER

The first time at Nancy's up in Maine
slow through fog along Crow Neck Road
Alan hunched tired over the wheel.
Fireflies call their lovers home.
We throw wood on the stove
Cook up waffles with wild strawberries & cream
coffee, lots of it
talk ourselves to the blink of sleep

In the loft I am wrenched back
by rain driving in from the ocean
a quarter off four
turn and fall in the soft of a borrowed bed

Piping of a whitethroat
coffee being ground below
I stumble down, pulling at my shirt
apple eggs warming on the stove
plates at the table set for three

I turn, Cathy, sense you at my shoulder
break awake loving you

MIRACLE MAN

Rain is everywhere.

The barn awash at its moorings,
An army of pine borers drills
The loft walls where
I sway and sail the night.

Come morning the rain gauge is full.
Five inches in some thirty hours;
Husks of pumpkin flop from the garden,
A tangle of orange buoys. Lost,
The dogs paddle out and back.
Wings glistening like heavy plastic,
A blue jay skids startled off the woodshed roof.

We crowd the kitchen with excitement:
Six a.m. and the vain promise of early light.
Truly, this morning we are walking on water.

And because it is what we have learned
We hold our breath against ghosts of rainbows
Hung along the soughing of the wind.
Do nothing until there is nothing left to do.

Unceasing, it falls three days more,
Sweeping from the ocean, a moving wall
Of water stripping trees along the north-east shore.
The road to the island is washed away,
The car caught fast by its axles and held.
Food is rationed; each trip
To outhouse or well measured in need.

This is the stuff to sluice away
Romance and miracles, caught like seeds
In a swirl of topsoil and flushed
Along the channels of the field
Clean to the clamflats of the bay.

THEN, LAST TIME

The anticipation was best. Mary, Molly, Judith and herself
arm-in-arm to the packhorse bridge, then, chattering,
barefoot and single file along the river, skirts wet
and heavy with mud, shoes soft in their reddened hands.

Before ever they saw the lights, the band,
cornet and organ, snap of the drum. Lads loitering
by the entrance, cigarettes cupped low at their side,
nudges and words, warmth of their mouths.

Laughing, they swept past them to the spin
of a hundred pairs of hired skates, round and around.
Linked tight they swirled and danced and sang,
all four, till breathless they collapsed,
a gawky, giggling heap into one another's arms.

Outside for air, he tapped her on the shoulder.
Molly, Mary, Judith, none of them were there.
She knew him from the weavers' cottages by Blackshaw Head
First time he kissed her their teeth clashed — so simple,
showing her the warp and weft to set it right.

The steps towards the common slippery and steep; they lay
in the lee of the wall, the moon masked above his face.
It hurt no more than two months later, when what they had made,
with no less a flow of blood, slipped out.

Between this Saturday and the next the country was at war
and before she could learn his name, along with all his mates,
he'd volunteered, the rink had closed its doors and though
sometimes she dreamed she saw neither one of them again.

TENNESSEE PLATES

Short of Chattanooga
they pulled over for
coke and gasoline
and he bought them
while she was in
the ladies' room —
glazed like eggshell
rough-edged round
in blue

Here — pushing them
into her hands —
Gotta have something
to eat off, don't we?
First things they'd
owned together
five bucks the pair
with gas

Mostly they stood
either side the mirror
leaning back on
little doohickeys
he made from wood
that winter he was
first laid off

Taking them down
to dust
rough and cold
against her cheek
all she could feel

One chipped short
of Thanksgiving
slipped through fingers
greasy from pecan pie

The other he hurled
against the wall
smashed into half
a hundred pieces
before storming
that last time
down to the lot
behind K-Mart where
he remembered a trick
he'd learned at school
hot-wired a car
and drove down
Highway 11 in a
blue and white
convertible
with Tennessee plates

SUNSETS

'Grandad looks like John Wayne,'
my daughter said, pirouetting away.

In the westerns I wrote he filled in corners —
the stage coach driver, the friendly sheriff
with spreading paunch and bowed back,
his holstered gun never drawn in anger
yet stubborn as a mule when the chips were down.

In photographs he holds me high above
his head like a talisman: pride bright
in his blue eyes I could never fulfil.

Writing, he stands between my sentences:
bits of a life catch like grit in the mouth.
Once I ran, sobbing, after him until
he swung me, safe, in his arms —

He stands in all the doorways of my childhood.
Stands between two trees, patient.
Stands for my meanness, my grudging thanks,
my shifts of direction which push him
further and further behind — driving home to visit
I had passed him on the road before I realised,
stooped and suddenly slow, one leg turned sideways
and dragged behind, an old man I had failed to recognise.

Laughter and meaning clogged thick in his lungs:
they moved him into a private room and fitted
a green mask fast over his face.
Each breath rattled dry stones along the bed of his throat,
his mouth peeled back and back until it disappeared.

Yet a week or so before he died,
the old smile alive for a moment in his eyes,
he beckoned the prettiest nurse and as
she bent to catch his words, nuzzled
the hard plastic of his mask against
her face to steal a kiss:
an act of imagination great
as any John Wayne ever made.

FLYING HOME

I remember the blitzkrieg of pans
that clattered and fell from the top
of the tall thin cupboard in my great
aunts' flat that summer we visited,
my mother and I, the year before
the war ended, the year I was five;
and the bomb, loosed by an airman lost
and turning back across the Channel,
landed close to two wool shops and the ABC
and close enough to us to free my aunts'
theatrical cries and scurry from their minds
all thoughts of scones and tea.

But who was the man, who, later that same afternoon,
appeared along the promenade in perfect time
to push my mother first and then myself
safely beneath the struts of a wooden seat
as a German plane flew low enough to strafe the beach?

And whose face, stubbornly kept amongst so many
of my father and myself, brown eyes and soft moustache,
the corners of his uniform well-pressed and neat,
unspoken of, unspeaking and so still?
Long afternoons when the radio would play Semprini,
say, and I was seven then, or eight, or ten,
the pages of my mother's book of photographs would turn
and turn and when it stopped, her finger to the page,
I would sense my father's sudden brace and glance
towards the opening door, the breath caught on the air,
a footstep in the hall.

SHE EXPLAINS IT ANOTHER WAY

for Lee Harwood

As if horsemen appeared
nudging the edge of the frame

The slight squeak of the rocker
stills on the porch out of sight

Dust across the sun
& the way their clothes
stuck to them as they came
towards the house

My father's words not quite
looking at me as he spoke

We would leave after a meal
carefully prepared   glazed
ham   pitchers of water
misting the glass

This stranger stands a way off
smoking a cigarette

'He is a fair man
you will see . . . '

　　　　She explains it another way

　　　　When my mother was nine years old
　　　　she got off the train at Colchester station
　　　　a hand at her back moving her across the platform
　　　　to where a man was waiting

A man seen through steam
(I suppose there was steam)
stepped hesitant towards her
(I hope he was hesitant)

'You are going to live with your father now'

('He is a fair man
you will see . . . ')

As if horsemen appeared
slow across the centre of the frame

We rode for three days
through country that refused
to dip or fall   hills in a smoke
of cloud to the west inter-
changeable

Owning it, he smiled

He performed his duties
handsomely   polite
nicotine on his hands

(I hope he will be hesitant)

The house square behind its arch
not a little impressive and between
the outbuildings the scurry for his return

Smoke from the chimney (there
was smoke) caught still
against the patina of sky

He helps me down

She explains it another way . . .

PAPER THIN

The room we put you in
large enough but only just
to hold the bookcase
you'd insisted we bring —
how else to hold those years
whose pages you could barely
read or turn?

There's television, matron
said, each room. And you
could hear your neighbours'
radios quite clearly
through the walls.

Each time I called
your fingers scraped
along the sheet
like dreaded mice.
You bent your head and talked
of wanting a new winter coat,
a perm, a pair of gloves —
of bits of girls who would
not help you dress.

Your skin slowed towards
the milky greyness of damp clay.

Several times you thought
I was my father, once my son:
to each of us confessed
you'd give life best.

When at last the phone call came
I sat and watched unrecognised:
your hair had dried like grass left
in the hiss and stale of hollow breath.
Before I walked away I touched your hand
but not your face, afraid the pressure
of a kiss might cause the skin to break.

AN END OF WISHING

Like a character in an Ida Lupino movie
she had all the moves: base line to main line
in three sharp years.

so much hangs on the outswing
of her curve
red bandanna
blue of her shirt beaten black
with sweat

on a cold night in England
as her opponent waits
she lifts her head away
from the trees
foot-faulting in someone else's shoes
imagining other places
other names that she might choose.

'It's bad when you're sixteen,
but when you're forty, it's no better'

the only thing is to keep the ball in play
& when the chance comes,
smash it hard as you can

Hard, Fast & Beautiful

MOVING ON

What happens, one day
pushing sixty, you're dead
& here I am with this child,
13, and me on my own?

The light in this room
a perfect light, always;
orange slides across
open space, & gold. Wood,
bowed and stretched, fits
snug against the winter,
sits tight onto the sash.

The old music: naked
in the window's bay
we sing each song
as if remembering —
as if remembering
each chord flush
against each chord.

What happens?

Out on the street
we stared up at the rain
as if we had never seen
rain before.

No reason to move
we settle china
into straw-bound boxes
sort old letters
pick at space & time
till there is little
more to heft against
the day

This much is certain.

TEMPS GREATEST HITS VOL II

'Are you in love? Is it going badly?'
'I'm always in love. sooner or later it goes badly.'
— Bernard Malamud, *Dubin's Lives*

for David Kresh

I wake at two to the sound of your breathing,
slowly realise the sea has fooled me once more
shuffling back along the upgang shore

I get up and don't switch on the light:
a tideswell like moving bone

Like Monk fingering 'These Foolish Things'
from broken glass

Like train times clicking down

'This place smells of flowers
and I think it smells of you
but of course it doesn't'

Up here at night poems bloom like dark
beyond the window

Last winter in Amsterdam
applecake fumbling from our fingers
we chased the cold from canal to canal —
afternoon movies, the American Bar —
it seemed nothing but games & glances

foolish chances

The moment before it happened
I was looking the other way:
the perfect writer's pose

This is no 'apples' nor even 'sea'
though both are mentioned
this is not an exercise,
a way of sealing 'difference'

What hurts isn't the thought
of you lying in this bed/that bed,
his bed/her bed, loving/being loved.

What hurts is the image
I have never seen:
you are with a new lover
hand in hand down from the city
walking that walk
and
  oh, baby
      I ain't too proud to beg
         ain't too proud too plead

OKLAHOMA TERRITORY

Four or five times Jug lets the bottle fall
from his fingers till finally it bounces
down between the trombones, Russell
opening one eye mid-solo to see
a fifth of Johnny Walker slide to a rest,
buffing the shine of his patent shoe.

And later, the dance hall owner, who doubles
as Baptist minister, starts in on intoxication
and immorality, drunkeness and wantoness and
ends up witholding ten per cent of the band's take.

Russell takes it anyway, philosophically, fines
Jug a night's wages and lays out the last of several
last warnings. Back on the bus those not already
sleeping talk in stage whispers of offers from
Bill McKinney, Henderson, Jean Goldkette. When
the banjo player deals himself a pair of eights
from the bottom of the deck somewhere south of
Oklahoma City, no-one's got the energy to complain.

It goes on like that, more or
less, for ten or twelve days.

The marquee out front of the Wasita Theatre
in Elk City advertises Tom Mix in *King Cowboy*
and off to one side, Russell Grant and His
Midwest Rhythm Kings: One Night Only.

We're playing for dancing after the movie.
Which is when the girl comes up to us, Russell
and myself, not a girl at all, a woman, black hair

flecked with white, skin that could only come from
the reservation, boiled bones and plain dirt every
day of her life. She wants to sing with the band.

'Sweet Georgia' comes in too fast, falls apart
too soon and she stands there, staring down
at chicken feet wedged into borrowed shoes while
the farmhands and stenographers near the stage
settle in to enjoy her humiliation.
Russell speaks to her quietly, calls Jug front
and centre, sixteen bars of muted trumpet,
'I Can't Give You Anything But Love'.
This time the tempo's right, the crowd is quiet,
something about the voice, and when she steps back
from the mike, brass bass supple behind me, I play
the best thirty-two bars of alto sax I ever played
before or since.

Turns out she's got kids, a cabinful of cats and scrawny
dogs, an old man doing five to ten upstate, a father
going blind: she'll ditch them all to join us on the road:
eleven men and a book of hand-me-down arrangements,
stalking our own sweat ten months of every twelve.

Russell shakes his head: he doesn't put her down,
he's kind. A bunch of the boys and myself argue him into
a corner but there's no changing his mind. He knows
what it'd be like, one woman on the bus; knows what
he's got's trouble enough already.

After that, pretty soon
it starts to fall apart.

Two dates cancel out in Kansas; Jug gets a telegram
to join the Orange Blossoms Band at the Graystone Ballroom
in Detroit. At a stop-off on 44 someone breaks into
the bus and steals a tuba and the pants to our dress suits.
The rest of the saxophone section are last seen
thumbing a ride east.

I bum the price of hash and eggs from Russell and leave
him in the back booth dealing solitaire.
I went with him when I was but nineteen and now
I'm twenty-one and the last thing I want to see is the look
on my father's face when I walk back through the door.

Outside I take a smoke and already there are more stars
than I could hope to count. In not so many hours
my brothers will start putting on their work clothes
for another day. I can stand here, staring out and
waiting for the light and all there'll ever be around me,
whichever way I turn, will be just another shade of corn.

ATLANTIC CITY AGAIN

By ten he was sweating a little, wondering
if it would be the full works or maybe just the lemons

The blind three-quarters down, the Girl from Plan B
called reverse charge to ask about her cat, smudging
shadows round the door

There had been a time, seven or six years back,
he had told himself this was nothing
but a quick stopover, no time for the mustard
to dry on the plate, but he had started sitting
up late, the pavements had seized his feet
& just when he thought he'd have to quit
he'd noticed the lemons

The scent first, soft-skinned and sharp,
like the skin of the girl down the study
hall he'd once longed for but never touched
not even with his eyes

Cross-legged, the phone coiled wild, if she
rang again he'd hold the cat's head close
so she could hear it purr all the way to Denver

Or Amarillo

'What are you doing?' Bluegrass faint
down the line, he knew she was homesick
and his heart, like a dobro, missed a beat

Old men at corners where markets might have been,
snow brown at kerb ends, a battered handful of dimes;

bookstores and cafés the only warm places: in the
East Village, her hand had curled about her cup of coffee
like the drift of woodsmoke in flat lands

He had watched her hour on hour:
she had never seen her beauty in his eyes

His notebook was across the room and he
knew she was never coming back: the light
through the shades flicked the sweat alive
and he leaned forward till his hands made
patterns on the hardwood floor. The room
spread out around him like grass.

Lemons: for a moment he could never remember
she crossed the light. Cat against his thighs,
brushing the wrong way. Tomorrow he would go
to the bookstore and steal a new book

Maybe the full works

NEIL SEDAKA LIED

'We should have a garage sale,' you said.

I grunted the way I had through
most of that November, cramming junk
into the refuse bags you'd brought,
old magazines, books bought and
never read, crusted tins of paint.

I'd been at it for months,
a drawer here, a shelf there,
making space.

Too busy to ask if that was what
you wanted or why.

'Is this what it will be like,'
you'd asked. 'When we're living together?'
We were in the garden under the trees,
watching 'Hill Street Blues',
listening to Patsy Cline.

Sweet Dreams.

Not much on which to build a life.

It wasn't until we were heading east
from the city, a weekend away
dark through late fall fields,
last leaves behind the spiral of your eyes,
nothing now to do but fail.

You saw yourself, this year,
next year, pacing between
wide white walls of my making,
body pregnant and swollen
with the child I alone wanted -
sometime, never.

Like cold water slowly climbing
my skin I understand your going,
thump of your cases on the stairs,
you pour, with more than usual care,
the last cup of tea from the pot
put on your make-up, check the diary,
wind your watch. What happened
to your diffidence when I needed it most?

See: it is not so hard to do.

There are small spaces all over this house
like sores. When the day starts to fade
I wait for the sounds of your homecoming,
knowing that you will not come home again.

I do care about you. I just don't care enough.

That's it then. Right. Now over here . . .

CLEARING

Back at the hotel
a small, family-run affair
close to all amenities
a reputation for hospitality
and local specialities
they think about a shower
but slump instead on single beds
placed head to head, whatever
the tour guide had said
was inadvertantly missing
from the phrase book
and when finally they'd arrived
the Palace of Culture had been
locked and barred.
She thinks for a moment
or removing her dress
touching his mouth to her breast
but it is too hot, too cold
too liable not to succeed.
She opens her book
and starts to read.
The mist that has lain
across the airport since
they arrived shows little
sign of clearing.

MUTTON

No more than a bunch of hippy kids & bleeding hearts
travelling across America by Audabon bus
picking up credits in life sciences and why
the disadvantaged live close to the land.

Still the dog ran off the reservation after them —
out across the desert in a hundred yards of yelping,
one-fifty, more, till they pulled over and took him in,
teach him, maybe, something about life: new tricks.

Six months later when the bus slowed back onto
Navajo land — 'Here now, he's your dog. Followed
us out and now we've brought him back. Take him.' —
They stared at his new-found weight with hungry eyes.
So the kids bundled him back into the bus and
brought him out here to Maine, 70 acres and a cabin
two square meals a day. Not too much traffic
up the track from Crow Neck Road, still time to time
he'll take out after a car or slow-departing truck
but at the bend he'll stop & bark & turn back home.

Without reason he'll stand afternoons between
the amber punctured pumpkins and the barn,
stare off into the distance, sound off for an hour
at no more than the echo of his voice.

But most of all he loves to slow walk under
the gaze of herons down into the edges of the ocean
and lay his belly in the fastness of grey mud;
to sit on rock and stare out at clam fishers
and yellow-legged waders, at what to him is still
a mystery: the sloping islands, the vastness of the sea.

LEAVING ON YOUR MIND

for Charlene Hooper and her Shooting Star Band

That crazy Connors kid torched
Four places till they caught him,
Hunkered down in some backyard on Third,
Watching last year's paint job burst
And blister, matches still in his hand.
Just another summer home so who's to worry?
Cuffed, they shipped him to the city,
Laughing fit to beat the band.

Out on County Road teenagers
Lob rocks at cars; a blind dog
Chases ducks the length of Main;
Dead seal on the beach —
All the excitement you can handle:
All you can expect to get.

Up on stage at the Lobster Pond
The singer's shoulders slump;
She is singing Patsy Cline to
Empty chairs and a half-dozen
Clam fishers a shot and a beer
Short of fighting drunk.
More practised than perfect
The band close round her and
Hit a waltz and she stands there
Still, staring out, the picture
Of what she is, sixteen.

Next day she wakes late and gets up later.
Her neighbour from across the street
Has already put in six hours at the smokehouse:
Split the herring, forefinger and thumb,
Splice it on a stick and lift,
Split the herring, thumb and finger —
Each season now these forty-seven years.

Her mother used to play the squeeze-box,
Pick guitar, she and her sister
Calling sets at Friday night dances
And fairs up and down
Hancock and Washington Counties.
Now the sister's moved away and
Her mother works at the market,
Hard-mouthed, afternoons from two till late.

There's a Molson left in the icebox.
She pulls on her boots and the leather
Jacket her father left behind. The
Scent of burning hangs sweet and hopeful
On the air. Crosstown she gives
The finger to a driver passing through,
Climbs a fence and walks round the
Deserted roller rink until she comes
Face to face with herself heading
The other way.

That night at the Blue Hill Diner
The band are passing bets she won't show.
But she's back there in the Little
Girl's Room, chair wedged against
The door as she fixes her make-up,
Shimmies her skirt over young hips,
Fringes at the hem and on her sleeves,
Sequins and bits of coloured glass,
Four-inch heels to her boots and a
Hummingbird right over her heart.

'Sweet Dreams'. 'Crazy'. One or two turn
Their heads to listen but it's not enough.
'I Just Don't Like This Kind Of Living'.
She stomps her foot, throws back her head.
She knows she has to make this happen.
Her voice already raw, tonight
She'll sing till it bleeds.

GHOST OF A CHANCE

He plays the tune lazily,
pretty much the way he must
have heard Billie sing it,
but slower, thick-toned,
leaning back upon the beat,
his mind half on the melody,
half on the gin.

Between takes he stands,
head down, shrunken inside
a suit already overlarge,
cheeks sunken in.
He thinks of her, Billie:
already it is possible
he has started to bleed within.

From the control room, laughter,
but that's not the sound he hears;
tenor closer to his mouth,
he turns towards the doors:
unseen, not quite unbidden,
someone has just slipped in.

At the end of eight bars
he closes his eyes and blows.
After two choruses he will cover
his mouthpiece with its shield:
not play again.

WINTER'S TALE

The other thing about getting older:
the impossibility of leaving the house
without at least three false starts,
all those pockets to be patted,
the cat, gas, can't believe I've got the keys
even though they're right here in my hand.

My occulist told me I was fine as far
as the small print was concerned,
but out in the real world
I'm getting more short-sighted every day:
no wonder role models for middle age
remain so hard to find.

I should try, maybe, those late Shakespearean comedies,
or Woody Allen movies
where it's unspoken but agreed
each and every laugh comes pre-paid in guilt,
each movement towards happiness framed beyond reach.
'Don't go,' he says, her flight confirmed,
cases by her side.

Nevertheless, crammed that first evening
against the Criterion bar, your hands moving
all the time, mine touch your arm once,
twice — three times cannot be a mistake;
before we're fifty yards along the street,
so easy to talk, we stop our mouths
with that first kiss.

Is there nothing certain we can take from this?

There is the way we walk across the city
one of your hands jammed tight into
the back pocket of my jeans.

The way Willie Smith's alto glides around
too much each time Billie sings
'Too Marvellous for Words'.

I saw you eat a whole bag of tortilla chips
without one ever touching your lips.

'Be quiet a minute,' opening your A-Z,
'I want to know just where we're going.'

I watch you stoop to lace your shoes:
so far you're not even up to speed.

BLUE TERRITORY

Impossible to tell
why I keep coming back to this:
the blue that clusters high to one corner
the boxiness
almost neatness of it.
Your face, the way it lets
   the screen shine
   back on itself;
landscape of colour,
fields spread wide,
stones stacked high.
two boulders, orange brown,
   with slates on top.
Your eyes as Michael Caine
   and Barbara Hershey
   meet in SoHo
   by mistake or design
— anyone married to Max Von Sydow
needs all the fun she can get —
a painter, too, whose paintings
   you can guess at
   parchment patterns
   etched from some Nordic twilight
Show this man the sun
and he would disappear,
set his canvasses against this
and they would split and crack.

Such warmth.
Your hands.
O'Hara's 'Poem Read at Joan Mitchell's'.
Women walking past with flowers,

Orange and blue in constant flow,
Thin lines of paint run down
   like gold, like fireflies
            like dust of wheat
                     spread by the wind
The hair of the girl in the grey jumper
at the table opposite,
falling long past her shoulders,
arching her back and resting
   her upturned hand
against the turn of her chin
   offering her profile,
   and I am grateful
but still thinking of you
and wondering if I should take
   Lunch Poems
from my bag and browse
or sit a little longer
toying with my walnut cake
and listening to this dreadful
music they are playing —
   Rimsky Korsakov
   or is it Smetena?
Peasants dragging their skirts and sleds
through the mud of some interminable river.
I'd rather be home with you
listening to Lester play
   'These Foolish Things'
   with Teddy Wilson
or sipping a late evening espresso
   at the Bar Italia
and later wandering across the street
   to Ronnie's
to hear Stan Tracey or Pharoah Saunders
   or even Mongo Santamaria.

But I stay here long enough
for the blonde opposite
to greet her lover,
another girl and blonder,
and against the pane of glass
this almost perfect painting
reinvents itself
   and I know
how something in my blood would sing
   if you walked in
the way white light breathes
through canvas
surfacing the blue.

NOTES

LIGHT IN AUGUST
The quotations are from William Faulkner's *Light in August*.

CHARLIE PARKER IN GREEN SHOES
Without Frank O'Hara, Charlie Parker and New York City there would be no poems. In the middle of what was otherwise — for me — a truly awful evening in Chesterfield, I got to read this with the alto saxophonist — and poet — Keith Jafrate and, whatever it sounded like, it felt great. Thanks, Keith.

GRACE NOTES
Tenor saxophonist David Murray is one of the most prolific recording artists on the current jazz scene — someone's getting something right. Try, maybe, *Ming's Samba* or *Ballads* for starters. Contemporary playing with a strong sense of tradition.

CHET BAKER
fell to his death from the window of an Amsterdam hotel, Friday 13th, 1988.

HEART-WHOLE
The quotations are from Nathaniel Hawthorne's *The Scarlet Letter*.

1947
The year of Jacques Tourneur's classic film noir, *Out of the Past*, the one I didn't finish writing my thesis about. The imagery here is borrowed more from Chandler, the mood from James M. Cain, the image of the rolling heart from the John Garfield/Lana Turner movie of *The Postman Always Rings Twice*.

SHE EXPLAINS IT ANOTHER WAY
Frank O'Hara aside, the strongest influence on my poetry — especially the earlier pieces — has been Lee Harwood. This poem — written for and partly about my mother — is a sort of 'version' of two of Lee's poems — 'Landscape with 3 People' and 'When the Geography was Fixed'.

AN END OF WISHING
Researching a detective story some years ago, I spent time on the British tennis circuit with a fine player called Debbie Parker, whose stroke play was considerably better than the resulting novel — *Dancer Draws a Wild Card*, issued by Hale under the penname of Terry Lennox, whom crime readers will know is . . ? *Hard, Fast and Beautiful* is an Ida Lupino film about what

tennis can do to a girl. Ask Andrea Jaeger. The lines in the middle are spoken by Gene Hackman to a very young Melanie Griffith in Arthur Penn's *Night Moves*.

TEMPS GREATEST HITS VOL II
David Kresh wrote a wonderful poem — warm & sexy — called 'Temptations Greatest Hits', which appears in his Slow Dancer collection, *Bloody Joy*. It's better than this, but I tried.

OKLAHOMA TERRITORY
Lee Wiley, Kay Starr and Mildred Bailey were all part-American Indian; the first two came from Oklahoma, one of the states which would have been among the stomping grounds of those territory bands which toured extensively in the late 20s and the 30s, often losing their best musicians to better known orchestras who worked in the major cities.

ATLANTIC CITY AGAIN
Burt Lancaster again, staring through the shutters at Susan Sarandon, only this time in a Country & Western mix. Think Lyle Lovett, James McMurtry. Even Primal Scream. I've spent quite a lot of time, both as student and tutor, on Arvon Foundation courses and owe the Foundation and its various organisers a great debt of gratitude. This was written in one session, sitting up into the early hours at Lumb Bank, sharing a bottle of Scotch with Jacky Hall and battling with a delinquent typewriter.

MUTTON
lives with Alan Brooks & Nancy Nielsen at their cabin in Downeast Maine. 'The First Day of Summer', 'Miracle Man' and 'Leaving on Your Mind' have their beginning there too.

GHOST OF A CHANCE
is based upon the picture of Lester Young taken by the photographer Herman Leonard in New York in 1959, and reproduced on the cover. I've tried writing about it before — in the second Resnick novel, *Rough Treatment* (Viking: London, 1990)

BLUE TERRITORY
refers to a painting by the American abstract expressionist, Joan Mitchell, whose work — especially, for me, her use of colour — is amongst the most exciting and satisfying I know. It's beautifully reproduced in *Joan Mitchell* (Judith E. Bernstock: Hudson Hills Press, New York, 1988)

John Harvey was born in London and now lives in Nottingham. A teacher for twelve years, he has been a full-time writer since 1975, starting Slow Dancer Press in 1977. His own poetry has appeared in a wide range of magazines, including *Ambit* and *The Listener*, and in seven small press pamphlets. This is his first full-length collection.

John Harvey's most recent fiction — the Charlie Resnick crime novels — have been published by Viking and Penguin in this country and by Henry Holt and Avon in the United States. They have been or are in the process of being, translated into ten languages. He is currently adapting them for the television series, *Resnick*, which is being made by Deco Films & Television for the BBC. Recently he has adapted two A. S. Byatt novels, *The Virgin in the Garden* and *Still Life*, for BBC Radio, for whom he has also dramatised stories by Richard Ford, Bobbie Ann Mason and Jayne Anne Phillips.